I0813357

Praise for *Everyday Gospel*

"Paul Tripp's *Everyday Gospel* is a wonder. It's brilliantly written, clear, concise, Christ-exalting, true to God's word, enriching to the mind, encouraging to the heart, and overflowing with gospel grace. Every paragraph has the ring of truth. If you want a daily dose of God's life-giving wisdom and kindness, this book is for you."

Randy Alcorn, author, *Heaven*; *If God Is Good*; and *The Treasure Principle*

"This deeply nourishing devotional reader gives us what we have all come to expect and gratefully receive from Paul Tripp: wise bridge-building from the depths of Scripture before us to the depths of our hearts within us, always flavored with the hope of the gospel. This will be a heartening and life-giving journey for any who receive Tripp's guidance through the Scripture each day."

Dane Ortlund, Senior Pastor, Naperville Presbyterian Church, Naperville, Illinois; author, *Gentle and Lowly: The Heart of Christ for Sinners and Sufferers*

"*New Morning Mercies* has been on our living room book table for years, and *Everyday Gospel* will soon be joining it. I encourage you to consider doing likewise."

Tim Challies, author, *Seasons of Sorrow*

"I need the gospel every day—not just a glimpse of it but the full depth and beauty revealed throughout all of Scripture. That's why I love this devotional. Paul Tripp brings the eternal truths of the gospel straight to the heart and shows us how to live in light of them. I hope many will use this resource and learn to walk in the good news of Jesus every single day."

Jeremy Treat, Pastor for Preaching and Vision, Reality LA, Los Angeles, California; Professor of Theology, Biola University; author, *The Crucified King*; *Seek First*; and *The Atonement*

EVERYDAY GOSPEL

Easter Devotional

EVERYDAY GOSPEL

Easter Devotional

PAUL DAVID TRIPP

CROSSWAY

WHEATON, ILLINOIS - ESV.ORG

Everyday Gospel Easter Devotional

© 2026 by Paul David Tripp

Published by Crossway
1300 Crescent Street
Wheaton, Illinois 60187

All rights reserved. No part of this publication may be reproduced, stored in a retrieval system, or transmitted in any form by any means, electronic, mechanical, photocopy, recording, or otherwise, without the prior permission of the publisher, except as provided for by USA copyright law. Crossway® is a registered trademark in the United States of America.

Cover design and illustration: Jordan Singer

First printing 2026

Printed in the United States of America

Scripture quotations are from the ESV® Bible (The Holy Bible, English Standard Version®), © 2001 by Crossway, a publishing ministry of Good News Publishers. Used by permission. All rights reserved. The ESV text may not be quoted in any publication made available to the public by a Creative Commons license. The ESV may not be translated in whole or in part into any other language.

Paperback ISBN: 979-8-8749-0905-5

ePub ISBN: 979-8-8749-0907-9

PDF ISBN: 979-8-8749-0906-2

Library of Congress Control Number: 2025945177

Crossway is a publishing ministry of Good News Publishers.

LB 36 35 34 33 32 31 30 29 28 27 26
15 14 13 12 11 10 9 8 7 6 5 4 3 2 1

CONTENTS

Day 25 *Luke 22:31–62*

Day 26 *Luke 23:1–25*

Day 27 *Mark 15:19–32*

Day 28 *Matthew 27:45–54*

Day 29 *Psalm 22:1–31*

Day 30 *Revelation 19:1–16*

INTRODUCTION

I don't know if you've thought about this or not, but the whole Bible is an Easter devotional. From Genesis to Revelation, Scripture records the story of God's plan to rescue us from the death-producing tragedy of sin. This is the central content of the biblical revelation. With all its drama and moments of seeming defeat, nothing can stop the biblical narrative from marching forward to its crescendo in the birth, life, death, resurrection, and royal priestly ascension of the Messiah, Jesus.

Over thousands of years, God recorded and preserved this amazing story for us because he loves us. He wants us to know that this story is our story, and in knowing, he wants us to be left in awe and wonder, brought to our knees in adoration and worship, causing us to live lives of gratitude, love, and surrender. The cover-to-cover Easter story of the Bible was not meant to be thought of so much as religious information. It was not meant to be treated as abstract theological information. There is one reason God went to the extent he did to preserve his story of grace for us: heart and life transformation. This story has the power to give life and to change you at the deepest levels of human understanding, motivation, and functioning. If you can walk away unchanged from the cover-to-cover Easter story of the Bible, you are a profoundly blind and deeply lost soul. No story has the power to do what this story can do because no story has a central character like Jesus, the Son of Man, the Son of God, the Messiah, who is God Almighty but comes to earth to be a servant and to give his life as a ransom for all who put their trust in him.

The Easter story is meant to confront us, expose us, comfort us, identify us, motivate us, and secure us.

Confront us. The way the Easter story works is that unless you accept its bad news, its good news doesn't mean anything to you.

This story confronts us with the inescapable truth that we are not okay. The words the Bible uses to describe us apart from God's grace are *lost*, *blind*, *wicked*, *rebels*, *idolaters*, *fools*, and *transgressors*, as well as other words like these. It is not a very attractive list! If you are any of these things, you are a danger to yourself, and your only hope in life and death is to be rescued from you. The Easter story is the story of that rescue. God confronts us because he loves us.

Expose us. This story serves as a great spiritual mirror. Like the mirrors we have in our homes, it is scarily accurate. Look into the mirror of the Easter story and you will see yourself as you really are. This story silences our ability to deny who we really are, silences our argument that we are okay on our own, and silences our hope that our righteousness is enough before God. God exposes us because he loves us.

Comfort us. A person who has been confronted and exposed needs to be comforted. The comfort of the Easter story is not rooted in flattery but in substitution. God doesn't work to make us feel good about ourselves; no, he comes to put himself in our place. He lives the righteous life we could never live; pays the penalty for sin in our place; rises again, conquering sin and death; and ascends to the Father to intercede for us. The comfort of the Easter story is a person, Jesus. God comforts us because he loves us.

Identify us. In the Easter story, God doesn't just forgive us; he gives us a brand-new identity. No longer known by our track record, our foolishness, our inability, our weakness, and our sin, we are now "in Christ." In Christ we are blessed with every eternal blessing, provided with everything we need, and indwelt by the empowering presence of the Holy Spirit. We are his new creation and nothing can separate us from God's love. This is who we are. God gives us a brand-new identity because he loves us.

Motivate us. There is no more purpose-infusing, empowering, and motivating story than the Easter story. Think about the fact that by God's sovereign plan, your little story has been embedded in the most wonderful story ever. And because it has, everything in your life has new meaning and purpose. You are now part of the grand army of redemption, and your choices, decisions, words, and actions matter in a way that they had never before. You can now live with courage and hope because Jesus has conquered sin and defeated death on your behalf. What is there to fear? God motivates us with his grace because he loves us.

Secure us. The first resurrection of Jesus carries with it the promise of a second resurrection for all who believe. This story will not end until all God's children have risen out of this evil world, with all its suffering and death, until every last tear has been dried, and until we are with our Lord in a world of peace and righteousness forever. God secures our destiny because he loves us.

So, this Easter, take time to meditate and luxuriate in God's grand story of redeeming grace. Don't just let it inform you; pray that it will once again transform you. It has been preserved for you because your Lord really does love you.

PAUL DAVID TRIPP

June 24, 2025

DAY 1

GENESIS 6:1–8

*Redemption is where God's anger with sin
and his grace toward the sinner embrace.*

It is so easy for us to minimize our sin. It's so easy for us to be more concerned about or irritated by the sin of others than we are our own. It is so easy to argue for our own righteousness while being judgmental and condemning toward the sin of others. But if you minimize your sin, then you will no longer value, seek, or celebrate the forgiving, reconciling, transforming, and delivering grace of God. If you defend yourself in the face of conviction, you are defending yourself from the best gift that has ever or will ever be given: redeeming grace.

One particular passage powerfully depicts the sinfulness of sin. These are the words of a Creator who is grieved by what sin has done to his world and to the people he made in his own image.

> The LORD saw that the wickedness of man was great in the earth, and that every intention of the thoughts of his heart was only evil continually. And the LORD regretted that he had made man on the earth, and it grieved him to his heart. So the LORD said, "I will blot out man whom I have created from the face of the land, man and animals and creeping things and birds of the heavens, for I am sorry that I have made them." (Gen. 6:5–7)

What a devastating explanation of the horrible nature of sin: "Every intention of the thoughts of his heart was only evil continually." Since the heart is the control center of one's personhood, for every intention of the heart to be constantly evil meant that the control of sin over people's lives was both total and inescapable.

How bad is sin? It is an inescapable evil that lives in the heart of every person who has ever taken a breath. Stop now and permit yourself to mourn. Let yourself shudder at the power of the anger of God with sin, an anger so deep that he decides to wipe out humanity from the face of the earth. Today, remember how sinful sin is in the eyes of the one perfectly holy person—Jesus—who has ever existed.

It would be terribly sad if the biblical story ended here. The very first word that follows Genesis 6:7 is *but*. Judgment would not be the end of the story. God would not minimize sin. He would not turn his back on iniquity. Through Noah he would extend his mercy and gather a covenant people, and through them he would raise up a redeemer.

In the story of Noah, the anger of God with sin and the mercy of God toward sinners embrace. Here we get a hint of the cross that is to come. It is the anger of God with sin that drives Jesus to the cross. It is the grace of God toward sinners that leads Jesus to the cross. On the cross of Jesus Christ God's anger with sin and his grace toward sinners embrace, and still today that is the best of news.

REFLECTION

Is there sin in your life that you are currently minimizing or attempting to hide? If so, confess that sin to God and be reminded of the redeeming grace of Jesus.

PRAYER

Lord, help me not to minimize my sin. Show me the ways in which I have broken your law and transgressed your boundaries. I praise you that you have sent Jesus, our Redeemer, to save me and all those who place their faith and trust in him. In Jesus's name, amen.

DAY 2

GENESIS 22:1–14

When life seems to make no sense, we are not without hope or help because we are the children of God.

I was facing my sixth surgery in two years. For me, it was a moment of irrationality. Life didn't make sense anymore. This surgery was going to be much harder and more painful than the others, and it would require a much longer recovery. If you have a surgery every four months, your body doesn't have the time it needs to recover before the next surgery. My body was weak and worn down. I wasn't able to sleep well and had little energy to face the day. I had the most wonderful ministry opportunities I had ever had. I had more gospel influence than I thought I would ever have. I looked around and saw so many places that needed gospel explanation and application. But I simply had no strength. It made no sense that I would be in the moment of my greatest ministry influence and yet physically unable to do what I had been called and gifted to do. Where was God? What was he doing? What had he given me for this moment?

Such was the life of Abraham. The miracle son, Isaac, had been born. God had been faithful to his promise. But now, in a shocking turn of the story, God asked Abraham to sacrifice the promised son (Gen. 22). It seemed like the cruelest trick ever: Build hope and destroy it in a moment. Here is life seeming to make no sense at all. In recounting the story, Hebrews tells us that God was testing Abraham (Heb. 11:17–19). This was not a test where Abraham would get a pass or a fail. This was like the tempering of metal, heating it to a high temperature to make it stronger. In asking Abraham to sacrifice Isaac, God was not doing something to him but doing something wonderful *for* him. God was building the faith of Abraham by proving his willingness to obey God no matter what and by giving Abraham the opportunity to experience the faithfulness of God's provision in moments of dire need.

You see, from the perspective of Abraham's covenant-making and covenant-keeping Lord, this seemingly senseless moment was a very sensible part of his plan for Abraham and all who would be blessed through him. And it needs to be noted that in this difficult moment Abraham was not without hope or help. Because he was a covenant son, Abraham possessed powerful, life-changing treasures. What did he have? He had the clear command of God, he had the clear promise of God, he had the blessing of the presence of God, and he was blessed to be the object of the infinite power of God. Abraham was not without help or hope because he was not alone.

The story of the near-sacrifice of Isaac points us to the sacrifice of another promised Son, Jesus. This Son died so that we too would be blessed in moments of need with God's presence, power, commands, and promises, always having the help and hope we need, even when life doesn't seem to make sense.

REFLECTION

In what way is this episode a "test" for Abraham? How did Abraham pass the test? Did God ever intend for him to kill Isaac?

PRAYER

God, help me to cling to your commands, your promises, and your presence. Remind me that I am never alone—envelop me in your Spirit's love. In Christ I pray, amen.

DAY 3

EXODUS 7:1–7

No story is more humbling, more beautiful, and more hope-instilling than the biblical story of redemption.

If someone were to ask you what the Bible is about, what would you say? How would you describe the content of God's word? What would you tell people to convince them that the Bible is the most important book ever written? The Bible is more than a history book, a theology book, a book of practical everyday wisdom, or a book of hope for troubled times. The Bible is essentially a grand origin-to-destiny narrative. It's God's story, accompanied by his explanatory and applicatory notes. One big theme holds together all the different parts of the Bible and all its different genres of literature. That theme is the theme of redemption. The Bible is the story of God's unleashing his power in order to provide the one thing that everyone needs: redemption. We need to be redeemed not just from the trials of life or our inadequacies or our weaknesses. No, we need to be redeemed from our sin. The main target of God's redeeming grace and power is not something outside of us, but something dark and destructive that lives inside of us.

The biblical story is marked by moments when God unleashes his redeeming power, so that his plan marches on until sin is finally and completely defeated and peace and righteousness reign on earth forever and ever.

The liberation of Israel from Egypt is one of those redemptive moments. The children of Israel cannot be exterminated in Egypt because the Messiah must come out of Egypt to provide final redemption for the chosen children of God (see Hos. 11:1). God demonstrates his lordship over every aspect of creation by unleashing his power in ten mind-blowing plagues. He is a covenant-keeping King, and he will do whatever is necessary, in his incalculable might, to deliver his children. This demonstration of his almighty power makes it clear that he will not abandon his promises. His will will be done (Ex. 12:33–42).

You have to stand as a witness to this incredible physical display of the enormity of the power and rule of the Lord and ask, "Who is a God like our God? Who loves his children like our God? Who is faithful like our God?" As you stand in awe of this picture of the power of God's redeeming mercy, it is vital to remember that in this moment God is not just moving to redeem Israel from its slavery in Egypt, but he is also moving to redeem us from our slavery to sin. If there had been no redemption from Egypt and no delivery to the promised land, there would have been no Messiah born in Bethlehem to live a perfectly righteous life, die a substitutionary death, and rise victorious over sin and death. All the redemptive moments in the Old Testament are not just for the people at the time, but they are for us too. In each moment God is fulfilling the promise he made in Genesis 3 that he would send a Redeemer to crush the head of the serpent, defeating sin and death. The story of the plagues is your story. The redeeming grace is not just for the Israelites back then but for you right here, right now.

REFLECTION

How has God redeemed you from slavery? What difference does this make in your daily battles against sin?

PRAYER

I extol you for your redeeming grace, oh Lord! I am in awe of your mercy and kindness to your unworthy people. Thank you for accepting me in Jesus, in whose name I pray, amen.

DAY 4

EXODUS 12:1–13

The radical, unexpected nature of the biblical story is that the hope for the Israelites in Egypt and our hope today rest on the shoulders of a Lamb.

It is a major understatement when the Bible says that God's ways are not like our ways and his thoughts are not like our thoughts (Isa. 55:8). No human being, no matter how brilliant, insightful, or experienced, would have been able to write the grand biblical story. The way God chooses to work and the instruments he chooses to use surprise us again and again. The apostle Paul expresses it this way: "God chose what is foolish in the world to shame the wise; God chose what is weak in the world to shame the strong; God chose what is low and despised in the world, even things that are not, to bring to nothing things that are, so that no human being might boast in the presence of God" (1 Cor. 1:27–29). God intentionally does things in a way that defies human understanding, explanation, and credit-taking. He works in ways that cause us to step back and say, "Only God could have done this," and in saying this, humbly run to him for the help that he alone is able to give.

Such is the story of the final emancipation of God's chosen children from Egypt. Despite Pharaoh's resistance in the face of the terror of the plagues, God would not grow weary, and he would not turn his back on those who were the object of his covenant promises. He would deliver. No one would stand in the way of the divine and holy will of the King of kings and Lord of lords, not even the most powerful ruler on earth. But the way the people would be freed could never have been anticipated by any Israelite. By God's wise and holy plan, the Israelites would be saved from slaughter and emancipated from their bondage by the blood of a lamb. That blood, sprinkled on the doorpost of an Israelite house, meant that God would pass over that house. God chose a lowly but spotless lamb to provide both salvation from death and liberation to a new life for his covenant children (Ex. 12:3–7).

Our hope, too, rests on the shoulders of a Lamb. Jesus didn't come as a conquering general, to throw down the kingdoms of men. No, he came to be a sacrificial Lamb. He, too, was a Lamb without blemish, who would be sacrificed for the salvation and liberation of all who believe in him. By the power of his shed blood, we are delivered from our bondage to sin and death and liberated to a new life of freedom as the children of God. We never could have written this story. We never would have anticipated that death would be the portal to life, that God would send a Lamb to do what kings, queens, and generals could never do. Now, that's a radical story, but it's very, very good news.

REFLECTION

Why was Jesus's death for our sins something "only God could have done"?

PRAYER

Lord, I seek you and call upon your name. Please forgive me of my sins and have compassion on me. I praise you that your thoughts and ways are infinitely wiser and better than mine. Thank you for sending your Son as the sacrifice for my sins. May he be my only comfort and hope. I pray to you in his name, amen.

DAY 5

EXODUS 25:1–9

True and lasting hope is found in these words: "I will dwell in the midst of my people."

There are a myriad of websites and media series dedicated to home decorating. Whether we are conscious of it or not, we are all very particular about how we want our home to look. Some of us take the look of our houses seriously and invest time and money to get them to look like our dreams. Others are more casual about our surroundings. Some of us place a high value on neat and clean; others find a bit of a mess more comfortable. But all of us somehow, someway express our personalities and our values by the way we design and keep our surroundings. That's why, when you are in someone else's home, it doesn't quite feel like home to you.

In Exodus 25 and the chapters following, we find directions for constructing and decorating a most important house: the house of the Lord. Read these amazing words carefully: "Let them make me a sanctuary, that I may dwell in their midst. Exactly as I show you concerning the pattern of the tabernacle, and of all its furniture, so you shall make it" (Ex. 25:8–9). You should be filled with wonder as you read these words. How could it be that the great Creator, the Sovereign King, the Holy One of Israel would ever desire to dwell among these sinful, complaining, and often rebellious people? Here again we are confronted with a major theme in the biblical story. God pours out his love on his people not because of what is in them, but because of what is in him. Nothing argues more strongly for the amazing and undeserved nature of God's grace than God's commanding his people to make a tabernacle so that he could dwell with his people. The hope of Israel was to be found in one place and one place alone: the Lord of glory and grace who lived among them.

But there is more. I don't know if you noticed it or not, but God not only said he would dwell among his people, but he also communicated that he was quite particular about how his house would be built, furnished, and decorated. He wanted his house to communicate who he was and what he valued. God wanted his tabernacle to communicate two things: his unapproachable holiness and the mercy of his forgiveness. This means the tabernacle is itself a prophecy.

There would be another place where God's unapproachable holiness and his forgiving mercy would meet: the cross of Jesus Christ. Here in God's mercy plan, the perfectly holy Lamb would die, so that we would become the children of God and so that he would come and dwell with us. A holy God, dwelling among his not-yet perfectly holy children, is our hope today too. What amazing mercy that by grace we have become the house of the Lord.

REFLECTION

How does the tabernacle point to God's dwelling with us permanently by his Spirit?

PRAYER

Lord, how could you possibly dwell with me? I am always aware of my sin. But thank you for Jesus, who took that sin upon himself at the cross. I laud you for your glorious plan of salvation in him. I pray in his name, amen.

DAY 6

LEVITICUS 4:27–35

No greater gift has ever been given than the gift of atonement for sin. We will be celebrating this gift of grace for all of eternity.

A sad awareness eventually washes over every parent. At some point, early in the life of your little loved one, you see sin rear its ugly head. It is obvious and unavoidable. You had hoped your child would be the exception, but it turns out she's not. She might refuse to do what you ask. She might shout "No!" to a command you have given. She might display selfishness or anger. You know the reason: your child is a sinner. It's not just that your child does things that are wrong. No, you are confronted with something profoundly deeper and more controlling. If the problem were just an occasional behavioral problem, perhaps some system of behavioral modification would work. But, as we look at every human being, we realize our problem is not just a matter of behavior; we have a problem with behavior because we have a nature problem. Sin is not only a matter of what we occasionally do. Sin, apart from the restorative power of God's grace, is who we are. We are sinners by nature, and that is why we have no ability to escape its power and penalty on our own.

I love the good news of Leviticus. This book in God's word is like a finger pointing us to where God's great redemptive story is going. Leviticus alerts us to the fact that God, in glorious grace, is very serious about providing atonement for sin. He makes a way for sin's penalty to be paid, so that gracious forgiveness can be granted. If sin is our deepest, most destructive, and most inescapable problem, then atonement for sin is the best, most-needed news ever. If you understand that every sin is a direct rebellion against God, then the gift of atonement becomes even more amazing to you.

Sinners offend God in innumerable ways, yet, with a love that is almost too wonderful for words, God moves to make atonement for sin possible.

Leviticus 4 uses a refrain three times: "The priest shall make atonement for him . . . , and he shall be forgiven" (4:26, 31, 35). These are glorious, hope-filled words. There is hope for us, no matter how strong the hold of sin is on us and no matter what dark hallways of sin we have walked. In these words we are assured that an utterly holy God makes a way for thoroughly sinful people to have their penalty paid and their record wiped clean. But there is more. In these words we find a promise of the coming of the Great High Priest, Jesus. He will be the final sacrifice, the complete payment, and the ultimate means of eternal forgiveness. What better news could you ever want to hear?

REFLECTION

What are several ways that the sacrifices in this reading point forward to the sacrifice of Jesus?

PRAYER

Gracious Lord, I confess my sin to you. Daily I break your law in thought, word, and deed. But thank you for Jesus, who has suffered the eternal penalty for my sin, in my place. Fill my heart with gratitude for his sacrifice! It is only through him that I can come to you in prayer. Amen.

DAY 7

LEVITICUS 26:40–45

Where would we be without God's forgiving and restoring grace?

It is important to have a well-oiled, activated gospel memory. It's important to require yourself never to forget. Few things are more spiritually benefiting than rehearsing the story of God's rescuing, forgiving, and restoring grace in your life. It's vital to remember that we not only experienced his forgiving grace at the moment of our conversion, but continually experience his grace as a lovingly patient process of restoration. God has forgiven you again and again, he has restored you to himself again and again, and he will continue to do so again and again.

God knows that between the "already" and the "not yet," living in a fallen world and with sin still inside of us, we will mess up. There will be times when we think, desire, and do wrong things. There will be times when we willingly step outside of God's holy boundaries. On this side of eternity we will sin. This is why God's commitment to forgive us and restore us is so beautiful and hope-inspiring. If you are at all humble, then you know you're not perfect. You know no day in your life is totally sin-free. You know you are a person in need of daily forgiveness.

God's forgiving and restoring mercies didn't begin with the birth of Jesus but were baked into his law.

> If they confess their iniquity and the iniquity of their fathers in their treachery that they committed against me, and also in walking contrary to me, so that I walked contrary to them and brought them into the land of their enemies—if then their uncircumcised heart is humbled and they make amends for their iniquity, then I will remember my covenant with Jacob, and I will remember my

> covenant with Isaac and my covenant with Abraham, and I will remember the land. (Lev. 26:40–42)

How does a person enter the blessing of God's forgiving and restoring grace? The answer, which is the same in the old covenant and the new, is clear: by humble, heartfelt confession. God will not turn his back on a sinner who comes to him with confession that is free from excuse or blame-shifting. He always greets the humble in heart with the fullness of his forgiving and restoring mercies. God has always been a God of grace, his people have always been in need of grace, and he has always reminded them of his willingness to respond to them with grace when grace is needed.

Leviticus 26 is yet another Old Testament passage that foreshadows the person and work of Jesus. These verses cry out for an ultimate and once-for-all purchase of forgiveness, for a sacrifice to be made that will forever restore us to God. Jesus has come to be that final sacrificial Lamb. In him our sins—past, present, and future—are fully forgiven. As a result of Jesus's work on our behalf, God is in us and we are in him forever, and nothing can separate us from his love. For sinners like you and me, there is no better, more beautiful gift than the gift of forgiving and restoring grace.

REFLECTION

What comfort do you find in this text, which upholds the promises of God despite his people's sin?

PRAYER

A broken and contrite heart, O God, you will not despise. Would you break my heart over my own sin? Would your Spirit assist me and intercede for me as I seek to confess my transgressions to you? Would you count me as righteous because of Jesus's death on my behalf? I come to you through him, amen.

DAY 8

NUMBERS 16:42–48

Jesus stands as the mediator between us and God. He takes God's judgment on himself, so that it will not fall on us. What amazing grace!

Some moments in Old Testament history summarize the entire redemptive narrative for us in one story. We need to pray that God would give us eyes to see these examples of redeeming grace and to understand that they are always about Jesus. In Numbers 16 we find ourselves at a shocking and sad moment in the story of God and his people. In holy anger God metes out judgment against his rebellious and complaining people. God will not compromise his high and holy requirements in order to have communion with his people. He will not allow challengers to his authority, faithfulness, or loving provision. In this moment we are reminded again that the wages of sin is always the same: death.

But this is not just a sad passage of holy judgment; it is also a beautiful portrait of God's provision of redeeming grace. Though 14,700 Israelites died, a tool of intervening grace spared the nation from being entirely wiped out. Aaron was the tool of this grace. He literally ran and stood between the dead bodies and those who were alive, with his censer filled with incense, to make atonement for God's people. Priests were never to come near dead bodies for fear of contamination, which would make them unclean and unable to do their priestly duties. But Aaron, as a tool of atoning grace, stood between the living and the dead, rescuing God's people from God's deadly and righteousness anger.

It should be impossible for us to look at Aaron here and not see Jesus. He is the greater Aaron, the Savior who comes to stand between the living and the dead. He not only makes atonement for the sins of his own; he is the atoning sacrifice. He not only is the Great High Priest; he is the Lamb of sacrifice. He not only stands between the living and the dead; he dies so that all who place their trust in him will live. Every act of atonement in the Old Testament is a finger pointing us to Jesus. The Old Testament is not simply a series of stories from which we can draw moral lessons. No, it is one story with many chapters. It is the story of the tragedy of sin and the progressive plan of God to provide a once-and-for-all sacrifice for sin, the Lord Jesus Christ.

The story of Numbers 16 confronts us with the fact that God takes sin seriously, and we should too. If sin is not serious, then there is no need for a Savior, but, if it is, then all of humanity is in need of Christ's willingness to stand between the living and the dead and make atonement for sin. There is never a day when you and I are free from our need for his atoning grace.

REFLECTION

In what ways are we like the rebels condemned in this chapter? Why do we not meet their same fate?

PRAYER

Savior God, although I deserve death, you have granted me life in Christ. I extol his name as my great priest and substitute, and I bow in gratitude for his atonement that has brought me peace with you. May my hope and faith always and only be in him. Through him I come to you now, amen.

DAY 9

DEUTERONOMY 21:18–23

The biblical story marches slowly to a man hanging on a tree: Jesus, who died as our substitute, the perfect sacrificial Lamb.

I wake up every morning with hope and joy. It's not because I always feel great. As I write this, I am in unrelenting pain. Something has happened to my back, which makes everything I do painful. Getting out of a chair is torturous. Riding in a car is agonizing. But my hope and joy are not diminished. My hope is not based on what God has called me to do. It does not rely upon people's opinions of me or my financial security. My hope is not based on the fact that I am married to my hero or that I have four wonderful children. My hope really does look back to a tree, outside of the walls of an ancient city, where an innocent man willingly suffered the cruelest and most humiliating kind of death, crucifixion, for the sake of my forgiveness, my reconciliation to God, my adoption into his family, and my eternal place with him in glory. Jesus is my hope. Jesus is the source of my joy. His work on my behalf, his presence, and his grace—not my suffering, my work, or my family—define me. My chronic pain does not make me angry or bitter, because I am daily blown away by the knowledge of what he has done for me and of who I am in him.

In Deuteronomy 21 God gives directions for how to deal with a man who has committed a capital crime, that is, one punishable by death. Such a person is to be hanged on a tree. It's a hard passage to read, but it is there for our guidance and protection. This passage sits in the Old Testament to remind us that God takes sin seriously, so we better take it seriously too. In order to have a relationship with his people, God never ignores or minimizes sin. This passage has been retained to remind us that something has to happen that will allow sinners to have a relationship with a perfectly holy God.

Deuteronomy 21:22–23 points us to two trees. First, it looks back to the tree in the garden of Eden, where temptation and sin first entered the world and separated people from their Creator. Second, it looks forward to that tree on the hill of Golgotha, where Jesus willingly suffered and died for our justification and eternal adoption into the family of God. In Deuteronomy, one man hangs because of his sin; on Calvary, one man hangs for the sins of others. In Deuteronomy, one man suffers the penalty for his iniquity; on Calvary one man pays the penalty for multitudes. One tree is a tree of death; the other tree is, ultimately, a tree of life. On one tree hangs a man who has no hope; on the other tree a man's death gives eternal hope to a countless company of sinners.

We have hope because of what Jesus did on that tree, and because of what he continues to do for us with mercies that are new every day.

REFLECTION

How can the law given in this reading motivate you to righteous and holy living in light of the sacrifice of Christ?

PRAYER

Dear God, may I never become numb to my own sin, or to what that sin cost you at the cross—the life of your only Son. May my heart and my life be reoriented around what Jesus accomplished for me there. May I hate my sin more and more, and may I love Christ more and more. In his name, amen.

DAY 10

2 KINGS 4:18–37

Christianity rises or falls on whether God has the power to raise the dead.

No power can compare with resurrection power, which God alone holds. It is one of the things that separates him from everything else. We are used to death being the end. This may seem crass, but when you attend a funeral, you expect nothing from the deceased. You know that there is no life in that person, and that is that. The finality of death is why it is so painful. Nothing leaves us feeling more helpless than death. Because sin ushered death into our world, and because death is the inescapable end that every living thing eventually faces, God's power to raise the dead is the ultimate victorious comfort to his people. The apostle Paul argues that if there is no resurrection from the dead, then the resurrection of Jesus is a fake, and, if that is true, then we have been duped and our faith is in vain (1 Cor. 15:12–19). The power to raise the dead is the platform on which everything we believe rests.

Three times in the Old Testament (1 Kings 17:17–22; 2 Kings 4:18–37; 13:20–21) and six times in the New (Matt 28:1–6; Mark 5:41; Luke 7:14; John 11:38–44; Acts 9:36–42; 20:7–12) someone is raised from the dead. Each of these has been recorded and preserved to remind us of the solitary power of God over life and death. The account of the Shunammite's son in 2 Kings 4:18–37 is the second recording in the Old Testament of someone being raised from the dead. God works this miracle through his prophet Elisha.

These nine accounts not only remind us of the almighty power of God, a power that not even death can defeat, but they also foreshadow where the story of redemption is going. Sin will not have the final victory. The story will not end in the unmoving stillness of death. Life will triumph over death. This is the plan of God.

The stories of individuals being raised from the dead that are sprinkled throughout the biblical story predict the necessity of two resurrections to come. The first is the resurrection of Jesus, after his death on the cross. He came not only to pay the penalty for our sin but also to defeat sin and death in his resurrection. Remember that the resurrection of Jesus is not the final resurrection; it is the firstfruit of resurrections to come. There will be a day when all the dead in Christ will be raised (1 Cor. 15:20). Death will die, and the children of God will live forever with the Lord of life, dwelling in his presence and basking in his glory.

The stories of these individuals are a promise of the greatest ending to a story ever imagined. In the dark valleys and hardships of life in this groaning world, we remember again and again that sin, suffering, and death are doomed. Someday they will imprison us no more, because with our Lord we will rise and breathe in the perfect air of the new heavens and the new earth, never again to shed death's tears.

REFLECTION

How does the resurrection of Christ ensure that his people will one day be raised as well?

PRAYER

God of Life, death has no dominion over you! I praise you for your power over the grave, for Christ's magnificent victory over all the powers of death and darkness through his death and resurrection. And I thank you for including me in that life, that I am born again even now and can look forward to eternal life in glory through Christ, in whom I pray, amen.

DAY 11

JOB 19:23–29

Amid all the questions, stresses, disappointments, and hardships of life, it is heartening to be able to say, "I know that my Redeemer lives."

Everybody has it, even people who consider themselves to be completely irreligious. It gets you up in the morning and motivates you throughout the day. It comforts you when you are sad. It gives you hope when your dreams have been dashed. It causes you to endure when suffering enters your door. You use it to encourage others. What am I talking about? Faith. Everyone looks to someone or something for security. Everyone has some kind of rock of hope. Everyone hooks his life to something he thinks is secure and will always be there. *Everyone has faith in something.* What makes Christians different is not that we live by faith. No, what makes us different is the *object* of our faith.

The things that most people have faith in ultimately will fail them. Only one source provides unshakable security and hope in this fallen world. If you want sturdy peace of heart and mind, quit looking horizontally and lift up the eyes of your heart. God is the only reliable, unfailing, never-changing, and always-faithful rock of security and hope. You can put your hope in him—not just because he has awesome power and makes wonderful promises, but because he rules over every situation and relationship you will ever have in your life.

This is where Job's heart goes in the middle of horrible suffering and loss, the faulty counsel of friends, and confusion about what God is doing. The words he speaks in the midst of his hardships have given strength and courage to generation after generation of believers. Job might not know and understand much at this point in his life, but one transformative thing he knows for sure:

> I know that my Redeemer lives,
> and at the last he will stand upon the earth.
> And after my skin has been thus destroyed,
> yet in my flesh I shall see God. (Job 19:25–26)

Speaking as a prophet, uttering words that have meaning beyond his understanding, Job reminds himself where unshakable hope and help can be found. What gives Job hope? God is alive and will never go away. After everything else has passed away, God will still stand. But there is more. Job knows that even though he is suffering, even though God has confused him, and even though God seems distant, God has not forsaken him and there will be a day when Job will see God.

Even if you're not facing hardship now, you will someday. In your tears and loss, may you look up with confidence and hope and say, "I am unsure of many things right now, but this I know for certain: I know that my Redeemer lives!"

REFLECTION

How can the knowledge that "my Redeemer lives" help you during hardships, even if it does not necessarily change those hardships right away?

PRAYER

O Great God, thank you for everlasting resurrection life! I exult in your victory through Christ over death, over decay, over destruction, over the devil, and over the grave. Lord, what other hope could I have besides this? May it fill my soul with wonder and joy. Thank you for Jesus, the eternal victor. I cry out in his name, amen.

DAY 12

PSALM 32:1–11

As a child of God, you receive the blessing of complete and final forgiveness.

What is the biggest blessing in your life? I know that I have been blessed in many ways. I have been blessed with a long-term marriage to my hero, my counselor, and my best friend, Luella. I cannot imagine what my life would have been without her. I have been blessed with four children, now adults, and the relationships of love we share with them. I have been blessed with six wonderful grandchildren. I have been blessed with a ministry life that has been more motivating and exciting than I ever could have dreamed. I have been blessed to always have food to eat and homes in which to stay. I have been blessed to be in wonderful churches that are committed to the gospel. I have been blessed with many faithful friends. I could go on and on with the undeserved and unearned blessings in my life, but one blessing is so amazing and life-transforming that I will celebrate it for the rest of eternity. This blessing gets me up in the morning and gives me hope. It has captured my heart and set the direction for my personal life and my ministry life. What is this amazing blessing that outshines every other on my list? Psalm 32 captures it well:

> I acknowledged my sin to you,
> and I did not cover my iniquity;
> I said, "I will confess my transgressions to the Lord,"
> and you forgave the iniquity of my sin. (Ps. 32:5)

We are all born in a condition so deep, dark, and destructive that it always leads to death. This darkness pervades every aspect of our personhood. We have no power whatsoever to escape it. It captures our heart and controls every thought and desire. It is the cause of every moral and relational human dysfunction. It makes life hard and sad. Sin is the worst thing that could have ever happened to us. Therefore, God's forgiveness is the best thing that could ever happen to us.

David uses three words to characterize this dark condition: *sin*, which is falling short of God's holy standard; *transgression*, which is the rebellion that causes us to step over God's boundaries; and *iniquity*, which is moral uncleanness. God's forgiveness covers each aspect of what sin is and what sin does.

It's an amazing blessing that we don't have to work to clean ourselves up or try to make ourselves acceptable to God in order to earn his forgiveness. No, he meets us as we are, asking us to come to him with humble words of confession and trust his forgiving mercies. Minimizing, denying, or excusing our sin never defeats it. Arguing for our own righteousness has never made us righteous. Comparing ourselves to others never breaks the hold that sin has on us. Our only hope in the face of this terminal disease is divine forgiveness. Psalm 32 looks forward to how that forgiveness will be finally secured for us by Jesus.

REFLECTION

How does examining and confessing the depths of your sin against God increase your gratitude for Christ's work? How should doing so affect your life from this point forward?

PRAYER

God, I praise you for your steadfast love. I bend in awe in the light of your magnificent mercy, which extends forgiveness even to sinners such as I. You are my hiding place. You preserve me from trouble. You surround me with shouts of deliverance. Thank you. In Jesus's name, amen.

DAY 13

ISAIAH 28:14–26

Jesus is our sure foundation. He is the cornerstone upon which the house of God stands.

When you're reading a well-written novel, you have no trouble identifying the main character. He will be there on page after page. He will dominate chapter after chapter. Although the book will contain many other characters and subplots, the novel really is his story. Everything in the book is somehow about him. If you were to take him out of the novel, the whole story would fall apart and make no sense, because he is the story.

So it is with the Bible. It is the story of Jesus. He is the hero of the story. His presence looms over every book of the Bible. You don't encounter him first in the New Testament. No, he is present from the very first chapter of Genesis (see Col. 1:16). As the history of the people of God is told in the Old Testament, sometimes it's clear that an author can be speaking only of Jesus, even though his name isn't mentioned. Isaiah 28:16–17 is such a passage:

> Thus says the Lord GOD,
> "Behold, I am the one who has laid as a foundation in Zion,
> a stone, a tested stone,
> a precious cornerstone, of a sure foundation:
> 'Whoever believes will not be in haste.'
> And I will make justice the line,
> and righteousness the plumb line."

The apostle Peter applies these words to Jesus (see 1 Pet. 2:6). In Isaiah, God is speaking into his people's present situation, but the words look beyond any human leader of the moment and find their fulfillment in Jesus Christ. Consider Peter's amazing description of Jesus. He is the tested stone. He faced Satan's temptations, the rejection of those he had created, plots against him, torturous suffering, and the general hardships of life in this fallen world, and he was without sin. Jesus is the precious one. There is no one like him. He is the gift of infinite value, the rarest of diamonds. He is the cornerstone of the house of God, the temple for the people of God, where his presence dwells. He is the definition of righteousness, and through his righteousness we are redeemed. He is the ultimate judge, who will restore perfect justice to the earth. When you entrust your soul to Jesus, he gives you everything you need.

Many of us live with cornerstone amnesia. We live in functional confusion and fear. The demands and busyness of life cause us to forget the sure foundation upon which our lives as his children are built. We forget that we are part of the surest edifice that has ever been built—the church, the household of faith. Although we face hardship, disappointment, and suffering, our lives are built on Jesus the sure foundation. We have a security that can never be shaken. Jesus is your cornerstone. What amazing grace!

REFLECTION

How is Jesus the precious cornerstone of his people? How is he your sure foundation personally?

PRAYER

Precious God, show me Jesus. Reveal your Son to me on every page of your holy Scriptures. Thank you for all that he has accomplished for his people—may his work be my only plea, my only hope, my only comfort. Build my life upon his secure foundation, that I may dwell safely in his presence forever. Through his name I pray, amen.

DAY 14

ISAIAH 53:1–12

Jesus willingly bore the penalty that we deserve, so that we can live forever in a reconciled relationship with God.

Familiarity with biblical passages is a good thing. By grace and through his Spirit, God works in us so that we will know and remember his word. But when we have read something many times, we might stop taking time to examine, consider, and be grateful.

You might be familiar with the following passage, but I ask you to slow down and take another look at some of its verses with me:

He was despised and rejected by men,
 a man of sorrows and acquainted with grief;
and as one from whom men hide their faces
 he was despised, and we esteemed him not.
Surely he has borne our griefs
 and carried our sorrows;
yet we esteemed him stricken,
 smitten by God, and afflicted.
But he was pierced for our transgressions;
 he was crushed for our iniquities;
upon him was the chastisement that brought us peace,
 and with his wounds we are healed.
All we like sheep have gone astray;
 we have turned—every one—to his own way;
and the Lord has laid on him
 the iniquity of us all. (Isa. 53:3–6)

If this passage doesn't shock you, I think you've missed its power. This passage is in the Bible so that you can understand Jesus's radical willingness to go through radical suffering in order that we could experience the radical intervention of God's grace. Jesus was willing to be "crushed for our iniquities" in order to secure our salvation. None of us would have accepted this job. But the King of kings was willing to be pierced, chastised, crushed, and wounded for us. He willingly carried the collected weight of all our sin to the cross. The eternal one was willing to die so that we could live forever.

Here's why remembering all of this is so important. If you forget or minimize the extent to which Jesus had to suffer in order to deal with your sin, then you will forget or minimize the gravity of your sin. If you want to know how serious, powerful, dark, and destructive sin is, then read Isaiah 53. Jesus had to endure all that he endured, including death, because that is how serious sin is. It requires a perfectly righteous substitute, one willing to face the temptations of life in this fallen world, suffer for crimes he did not commit, and die as a sacrifice for our sins.

Our hope in this life and the one to come hinges on the willingness of Jesus to endure what none of us would be willing to endure. He was willing. What grace!

REFLECTION

Why is this passage in Isaiah 53 so shocking? What do we learn about Jesus in these verses?

PRAYER

Savior, what suffering you endured for me! I bow in humble adoration and exultation that you would suffer to such a degree in order to redeem a sinner such as me! It was truly my sin that pinned you to the cross. It was truly my guilt that bruised your head. It was truly my unrighteousness that stripped your clothes and pierced your side. Thank you for enduring all of that—and more—for me. I love you. I pray in your name, amen.

DAY 15

ISAIAH 59:1–13

Humanity was created to live in a loving, worshiping, and life-giving relationship with God, but sin separated us from the one we were created to live with and for.

Most of us hate to be separated from those we love. Luella and I have three married children and six grandchildren in Southern California. So, though we live in Philadelphia, we have become bicoastal. We spend about half of our time in California and half with our married son and his wife in Philly. We love being with our grandchildren out west, and there are always tears shed when we leave. While we are in California, we miss our East Coast son and his wife and anticipate our time with them as we are flying home to Philly. Because we are not omnipresent, we are always happy to be with those we're with, yet sad because other loved ones are so far from us. Few things are more joyful than being among those with whom you share a deep bond of love.

But, even when we consider the immense sadness that human separation brings, nothing in life is sadder than being separated from God. Of all the tragedies we face in life, this is the tragedy of tragedies. Not only were we made by God, but we were made for him. Every person you see on the street, in a store, at work, at a conference, at a reunion, at church, or at a concert was made for a relationship with God. God designed us to find our highest end and purpose in him. Our relationship with him was meant to be the way we understand our identity. Worship of him was meant to be the deepest and most abiding motivation of our hearts. It was in relationship with him that we were meant to find our humanity and our sanity.

Therefore, the greatest tragedy is that people who were made in the image of God became separated from him:

Behold, the Lord's hand is not shortened, that it cannot save,
  or his ear dull, that it cannot hear;
but your iniquities have made a separation
  between you and your God,
and your sins have hidden his face from you
  so that he does not hear. (Isa. 59:1–2)

God hid his face from those he had made. How tragic! Separation from him means losing not only true spirituality but also true humanity. We cannot be what we were meant to be apart from him. Separation from him is our eternal doom. Sin is not just the breaking of moral law; it is the breaking of a relationship with God that was meant to be the core of who we are.

This is why we celebrate the life, death, and resurrection of Jesus. Through him our sins are atoned for, we are reconciled to God, and sin separates us no more. By grace he is ours and we are his forever. Sin has been defeated, so those who believe are separated from God no more. Now, that's very good news!

REFLECTION

Are you guilty of any of the sins described in today's Scripture reading? Which ones? Have these sins separated you from God? Why or why not?

PRAYER

God, Eternal Ruler of All Things, I recognize how my sin once separated myself from you. But thank you for breaching that gap, for reconciling me to yourself by the precious blood of your only begotten Son. May I never take for granted the relationship I have with you, the access I enjoy, the life I experience with you because of him. Thank you for turning sinners like me into saints, into your holy people, through Christ. I come now through him, amen.

DAY 16

JEREMIAH 50:8–20

By grace, the restoration that the world desperately needs is on its way.

It is hard to deny the fact that you and I live in a world that desperately needs to be restored. Just look at your media feed, or recall the sad things that have happened in your lifetime. The apostle Paul writes that we live in a world that is groaning, waiting for redemption (Rom. 8:22–23). You groan when you're in pain; you groan when you're tired; you groan when you're disappointed; you groan when things around you seem irreparably broken. Such is the state of the world in which we live. The violence around us takes your breath away. The moral degradation of the culture seems to go on unabated. The witness of the church often seems compromised. Marriages break apart, and parents throw up their hands in frustration at their children. Entertainment media have ceased to be a safe place of escape. Even the physical world around us groans. The world today is not as God created it, and it does not function as God intended.

We sometimes cry out, "God, are you there? Do you see what is happening? Do you hear our cries for help? Have you abandoned what you have made?" We feel weak and powerless, unable to bring about the massive change that is needed. And so we pray and hope. But prayer is not a final act of desperation by people who don't know what else to do. The Bible is punctuated with promises of restoration. These promises should remind you that God hasn't abandoned his creation. They have been recorded and preserved so that you would know that your prayers are not in vain. They assure you that restoration is written into God's unshakable redemptive plan.

We find such a promise in Jeremiah 50. It comes at a time when it looks as though things couldn't get any worse for the children of God. It is a shining light of hope in the darkest of times, sent by a God of love to comfort his children down through the ages:

> Israel is a hunted sheep driven away by lions. First the king of Assyria devoured him, and now at last Nebuchadnezzar king of Babylon has gnawed his bones. Therefore, thus says the LORD of hosts, the God of Israel: Behold, I am bringing punishment on the king of Babylon and his land, as I punished the king of Assyria. I will restore Israel to his pasture, and he shall feed on Carmel and in Bashan, and his desire shall be satisfied on the hills of Ephraim and in Gilead. In those days and in that time, declares the LORD, iniquity shall be sought in Israel, and there shall be none, and sin in Judah, and none shall be found, for I will pardon those whom I leave as a remnant. (Jer. 50:17–20)

God will crush evil and restore and purify his people. Evil will not win. Renewal is on the way. There's reason for hope.

REFLECTION

Think of temptations or troubles in your life that cause you to long for the renewing work of God. How does your hope in his restoration lead you to deeper love now for the triune God?

PRAYER

O Lord Most Awesome and Holy, I have hope because of you. Despite all the evil and wickedness all around me—and inside me—I know that you will not fail to judge the sin of this world. And I know that, for your people, you have already done so, placing our sin upon Jesus at the cross, that we might be forgiven, cleansed, and freed. Thank you for this glorious truth of your gospel, centered on your beloved Son, through whom I pray, amen.

DAY 17

LAMENTATIONS 3:19–26

No matter how stuck you might seem, something in your life is new every morning: the mercy of the Lord.

Do you feel stuck? Do you long for change? Does your spiritual life seem stagnant? Does it feel as though your hopes and dreams are in suspended animation? Is your marriage stuck in unhealthy patterns? Are your friendships mired in repeated conflict? Do your children seem stuck? Does your church seem stuck, never becoming the church you wish it would be? Are you trapped in sin patterns that leave you feeling guilty and hopeless? Do you seem stuck in your reading of God's word, never feeling that you walk away with renewed faith and hope? Are your finances stuck in patterns of debt? Are you tempted to give up on change?

In the darkest and saddest moments in the history of the people of God, God gives his children a reason not to give up. It's not because they are wise, capable, or righteous. He does not tell them that they have the power to turn things around. Through his prophet, God communicates the hope for change in just a few words: "His mercies never come to an end; they are new every morning" (Lam. 3:22–23). Here is where hope is found in this "stuck-again" world in which we live. God's mercies never grow old. They are never out of date. They are never inappropriate. They never lack power. They never run out. God's mercies never fail. Each morning the people of God are blessed with mercy from the Lord that is form-fit for the trials, opportunities, pressures, obligations, griefs, and temptations of that day. God's mercies are not sitting dusty in a warehouse. No, like fresh fruit, they are hand-delivered by the Savior every day. Each child gets mercy, but each gets just the kind of mercy he or she needs for that day.

It is also true that the steadfast love of the Lord never ceases (Lam. 3:22) and that his faithfulness is great (3:23). Therefore, we have reason to hope in the Lord. Your hope is never in vain, because God's mercies are always new. His mercies are always new because his steadfast love never ends. And his steadfast love never ends because God is the ultimate definition of faithfulness. Behind every new and needed mercy is a God of faithful, steadfast, and unceasing love.

The pinnacle of the new mercies of our Lord is the gift of his Son. Jesus lived, died, and rose again so we would have every mercy that we need: "The LORD is my portion," says my soul, "therefore I will hope in him" (Lam. 3:24).

Jesus is the new mercy of the Lord, now dwelling with his people with redeeming and restoring power. He is with you, in you, and for you with boundless mercy. He will not leave you stuck. You have reason for hope.

REFLECTION

How have you seen the steadfast love of the Lord in concrete or surprising ways over the past several days? Praise God for his undying commitment to you, and rest in his love.

PRAYER

How great are your mercies, O Lord! How glorious, how wonderful, how marvelous is your steadfast love to your people! Indeed, not a day goes by in which you do not lavish your kindness upon me and upon all your beloved people. You are rich in grace and affection. Therefore, I will hope in you. You have provided me all things in Christ, in whom I pray, amen.

DAY 18

EZEKIEL 37:1–14

Jesus is the resurrection and the life. He can make dry bones live—and that is the best news.

This famous passage in Ezekiel addresses the age-old question: Where do we find hope?

> Then he said to me, "Prophesy over these bones, and say to them, O dry bones, hear the word of the Lord. Thus says the Lord God to these bones: Behold, I will cause breath to enter you, and you shall live." . . .
>
> So I prophesied as I was commanded. And as I prophesied, there was a sound, and behold, a rattling, and the bones came together, bone to its bone. And I looked, and behold, there were sinews on them, and flesh had come upon them, and skin had covered them. But there was no breath in them. Then he said to me, "Prophesy to the breath; prophesy, son of man, and say to the breath, Thus says the Lord God: Come from the four winds, O breath, and breathe on these slain, that they may live." So I prophesied as he commanded me, and the breath came into them, and they lived and stood on their feet, an exceedingly great army. (Ezek. 37:4–5, 7–10)

When we consider the disastrous history of Israel, a people whom God chose, loved, guided, protected, and provided for, we might ask, Where is hope for these rebellious people to be found? They forsook their Father for other gods. Evil king after evil king led the people astray. God's people lost everything. Jerusalem and the temple were destroyed. And so we ask, Where is hope to be found?

It is clear that hope is not found in human righteousness, because that always falls short of God's holy standard. It is clear that hope is not found in human wisdom, because we are capable of so much foolishness. It is clear that hope cannot be found in human strength, because, in the face of sin and temptation, we can be so weak. Hope is found in only one place: the power of our Lord to bring dry bones together again and breathe life into them. Our God has the power to bring life out of what is dead. It seemed as though God's children were dead and gone—but reigning over Israel was a God who has resurrection power.

That God is your Lord. He has the power to resurrect your dry bones and give you new life. As in the Valley of Dry Bones, resurrection is an event, followed by a process. By grace, when we believe, we are raised to newness of life. Then, through a lifelong process and by means of sanctifying grace, God works to resurrect every area of our lives. Jesus declares himself to be the resurrection and the life, and he is in you and for you.

Where is hope to be found? In the awesome resurrecting power of Jesus, who came so that we might have life, full and eternal.

REFLECTION

How can you know that God has given you new life in Christ? What evidence do you see in your thoughts, words, or relationships?

PRAYER

O Lord, thank you for how clear your Scriptures make it that my hope is not found in any righteousness I could offer, or in any wisdom I could collect, or in any strength I could muster. I rest in your power to bring resurrection life to dry and dusty bones. I magnify your Holy Spirit, who has breathed new life into me. Thank you for Jesus, the true resurrection and life. In him do I pray, amen and amen.

DAY 19

NAHUM 1:1–8

No one can withstand the anger of the Lord; that is why we are thankful for his forgiving and reconciling grace.

The little book of Nahum begins with a heart-rattling description of the anger of God. This description has been recorded and preserved as a means of instruction and rescue. Often when people read through the Old Testament and encounter a description of God's anger, they wonder about or even doubt the goodness of the Lord. As you read through Scripture, notice that God does not hide his anger from us. He is not ashamed of his anger, as though it were a mortifying character weakness. It is impossible for God to have character weaknesses of any kind. If God is perfectly holy—and he is—then his anger is not a contradiction of his holiness, but an aspect of it. God could not be perfect in holiness and tolerant of the enormous evil of sin at the same time. Think about a time when you were sinned against, and those around you didn't seem to care. How did you feel? God's unending anger with sin is a constant demonstration to us of just how holy and good he actually is.

God reveals his anger toward sin again and again for good reason. First, God's anger with sin reminds us of how deeply evil and destructive sin is. We need this reminder because sin doesn't always look sinful to us. God's anger with sin is also a call to never minimize or deny it, but to run from it into his arms of grace. God's revelation of his anger with sin is meant to give us hope that there will be final justice, when sin is defeated forever. God's revelation of his anger with sin is also designed to cause us to love the rescuing wisdom of his commands. God's revelation of his anger with sin is meant to cause us to stand in awe of his holiness and to give him the worship that he deserves. But most of all, God's desire to reveal his anger is designed to point us to Jesus. Through Jesus's perfectly righteous life, substitutionary death, and victorious resurrection, God's anger is satisfied and we are no longer under its threat. On the cross of Jesus Christ, God's holy anger against sin and his tender heart of grace met. Jesus had to die because God could never compromise his holiness just to extend grace.

So when you read, "Who can stand before his indignation? Who can endure the heat of his anger?" (Nah. 1:6), know that you are being loved. God is warning you to take sin seriously, to never see it as beautiful, and to never think that on your own you can escape his anger with sin. In these words God lovingly reminds you of how much you need the atoning work of the Lord Jesus Christ. He took your sins on himself. He bore the anger of God in his own body. He endured the Father's rejection. And he did it all so that you may be reconciled to God forever.

REFLECTION

How does it feel to realize that the same sort of wrath described in this reading is deserved by us because of our sin? And how does it feel to realize that this is precisely what Jesus received on our behalf at the cross?

PRAYER

Holy Father, how easy it can be to be allured by the tantalizing attractiveness of sin. Thank you for using the stark pictures of your word to remind us of how deeply evil and destructive sin truly is. Cause your people to flee from sin and to run into your arms. Thank you for judging evil and sin—and for judging mine at the cross, where your perfect holiness and perfect grace met. Thank you for the sacrifice of Jesus. I pray in his name, amen.

DAY 20

ZECHARIAH 9:9–17

The Bible isn't an anthology of stories; it is one unified story. The Bible isn't a sampling of isolated promises; it is a collection of promises that all find their fulfillment in Jesus.

When you hold your Bible in your hands to do your daily reading, you should know what you are holding. Your Bible isn't a simple collection of stories with morals for your everyday living. Your Bible isn't a mere collection of wisdom principles to make your life better. Your Bible isn't a systematic theology textbook. Your Bible is the story of God's grand redemptive plan. It is a story with many chapters, but it is one unified story. Maybe the best way to say it is that the Bible is God's grand redemptive story, containing his explanatory and applicatory notes. Your Bible tells the story of how this world was created, how sin entered and damaged the world, how that will get fixed, and what the final end of all things will look like. There is one hero in the Bible. He is the one about whom the Old Testament prophesies, whose life and work the New Testament chronicles, and whose work the Epistles explain. Your Bible is the biography of Jesus.

You should read your Bible with its unity in mind. One of the places where you see this unity clearly is in the book of Zechariah. This book is one of the Old Testament books quoted most by New Testament authors. Under the inspiration of the Holy Spirit, these New Testament writers understood that the many prophecies made to Israel ultimately pointed to and would have their final fulfillment in the coming, the person, and the redeeming work of Jesus. They understood that the partial fulfillment of these passages in Old Testament times was not the end of the story. If, under the guidance of the Holy Spirit, they looked into the Old Testament and saw Jesus, then we should do the same.

One of the most striking and specific passages that finds its ultimate fulfillment in Jesus is in Zechariah 9:

> Rejoice greatly, O daughter of Zion!
> Shout aloud, O daughter of Jerusalem!
> Behold, your king is coming to you;
> righteous and having salvation is he,
> humble and mounted on a donkey,
> on a colt, the foal of a donkey. (Zech. 9:9)

Matthew quotes this passage on the occasion of Jesus's triumphal entry into Jerusalem, where he would be tried for crimes he did not commit, suffer and die for our sins, and rise again to ascend in victory to the right hand of his Father (Matt. 21:5). Jesus is the humble King. He comes not to set up an earthly kingdom, but to suffer and die, so that his kingdom may reign in the hearts of all who believe and so that his final kingdom may one day come. Zechariah writes of more than a promised earthly king. He writes of the King of kings, who is also the Lamb of sacrifice. Here in some of the final words of the Old Testament is gospel hope. We have the assurance that there is one hope in this life and the one to come: Jesus.

REFLECTION

In what ways was the cross a part of Jesus's work to establish an eternal kingdom?

PRAYER

Sovereign God, I delight in your prophecies of a gentle King who would come and rule his people. Thank you for coming to rule in the person of Jesus! May I be filled with hope and assurance, knowing that the one prophesied of long ago will come again to usher in his eternal rule once and for all. Grant me great joy as I await his coming! I pray in his name, amen.

DAY 21

JOHN 11:17–44

Surrounded by death and grief, Jesus proclaims, "I am the resurrection and the life."

Everyone who is familiar with the Bible knows the story of the raising of Lazarus. John gives this amazing story a lot of ink in his Gospel, but I want to focus on the conversation between Jesus and Martha after Jesus finally arrives on the scene—four days after Lazarus dies. For many Jews, the fourth day was important because it signified that Lazarus was officially dead:

> Now when Jesus came, he found that Lazarus had already been in the tomb four days. Bethany was near Jerusalem, about two miles off, and many of the Jews had come to Martha and Mary to console them concerning their brother. So when Martha heard that Jesus was coming, she went and met him, but Mary remained seated in the house. Martha said to Jesus, "Lord, if you had been here, my brother would not have died. But even now I know that whatever you ask from God, God will give you." Jesus said to her, "Your brother will rise again." Martha said to him, "I know that he will rise again in the resurrection on the last day." Jesus said to her, "I am the resurrection and the life. Whoever believes in me, though he die, yet shall he live, and everyone who lives and believes in me shall never die. Do you believe this?" She said to him, "Yes, Lord; I believe that you are the Christ, the Son of God, who is coming into the world." (John 11:17–27)

Martha's first words to Jesus are exactly what you would expect from someone who has witnessed the power of Jesus firsthand: "If you had been here, my brother would not have died." Jesus's response is both clear and radical: "Your brother will rise again." There is no hesitation or equivocation in these words. Martha misunderstands what Jesus is saying. He is making a present declaration, but what she hears is a future promise. Jesus is not talking about the final resurrection; he is talking about what he intends to do to Lazarus now. The Son of God knows himself and understands the power that is at his disposal.

What Jesus says next is glorious. He declares his identity, along with a summary of the hope of the gospel. "I am the resurrection and the life." Resurrection power and the giving of eternal life are inextricably connected to Jesus—and to no one else. So it is right for him to say, "I am the resurrection" and "I am the life." But Jesus is not done. He then says, "Whoever believes in me, though he die, yet shall he live."

Here is the gospel of grace. We are all born dead in sin, a condition we cannot escape. By grace, Jesus breathes life into all who believe. And even though believers still physically die, we will rise again and live with him forever. Standing before Lazarus's tomb, Jesus preaches to us his resurrection power.

REFLECTION

How do Jesus's words to Mary and Martha fill you with hope amid your daily struggles of life in this world?

PRAYER

O God, I confess my sins against you and your word. I acknowledge that I deserve only death because of the ways in which I have rebelled against my Maker and Lord. And so I bow in awe and gratitude for the grace offered to me in Christ, who has breathed life into me and promised me eternal life in him. I praise his resurrection power! Thank you for Jesus. I come to you in his name, amen.

DAY 22

PSALM 51:1–19

One of the best things you can ask of God is a clean heart.

Psalm 51 is a beautiful prayer of confession and repentance:

> Purge me with hyssop, and I shall be clean;
> wash me, and I shall be whiter than snow.
> Let me hear joy and gladness;
> let the bones that you have broken rejoice.
> Hide your face from my sins,
> and blot out all my iniquities.
> Create in me a clean heart, O God,
> and renew a right spirit within me. (Ps. 51:7–10)

David wrote these words after his sins of adultery and murder. He makes no excuses in this psalm, he does not minimize what he has done or shift the blame elsewhere, and he does not argue for his own righteousness. In verses 1–6 David acknowledges his sin and even confesses that this sin was not just a technical breaking of God's law; it was an offense against God himself. This is what true confession looks like. But at verse 7, the psalm takes a turn.

David has come to understand that he doesn't have just a temptation problem or a behavior problem; he has a heart problem. His actions went where his heart had already gone. So David needs the sort of forgiveness that only God can give—the kind that cleanses the heart. His problem was not that Bathsheba was beautiful; no, his problem was he looked on her beauty with an unclean heart. So he prays for something he cannot create on his own, something that requires divine intervention: a clean heart.

But David asks for something else. He prays, "Let the bones that you have broken rejoice." David acknowledges that, in order to reclaim and purify our hearts, God often leads us through pain and hardship. He does what we can't do for ourselves—create in us a clean heart. David is talking here about God's hammer of grace. Grace is not always a cool drink or a soft pillow. God's grace often leads us into difficulty and pain, not because God is evil or lacking in love, but in order to recapture our hearts. So, in perfect redeeming love, God may break things in our lives that capture our hearts and our worship. The beauty of a clean heart before God is far more valuable than bones that have to be broken to cleanse and free us.

Like all the psalms, Psalm 51 points us to Jesus. God was willing to bruise, break, and sacrifice his Son so that it would be possible for us, in Christ, to stand before him perfectly clean. Now he works so that we will be not just positionally clean before him, but actually clean. And he will not relent until every atom of sin is removed from every cell of every heart of each of his children. What grace!

REFLECTION

Although Jesus never sinned—not even once—how does he nevertheless embody David's words here in Psalm 51? How does this realization help you to appreciate the gospel better?

PRAYER

Heavenly Father, please grant me insight, that I may see how all my sin is, above all, sin against you. Help me not to minimize my sin or to blame others for it. I thank you that I may have confidence that all my sin has been washed away by the blood of Jesus! Thank you for his atoning work on behalf of all his precious people. I can come to you only through him. Amen.

DAY 23

MATTHEW 26:14–29

Jesus is the fulfillment of generations of Passover hope, because he is the Passover Lamb.

Exodus 12 records God's plans for the first Passover:

> It is the Lord's Passover. For I will pass through the land of Egypt that night, and I will strike all the firstborn in the land of Egypt, both man and beast; and on all the gods of Egypt I will execute judgments: I am the Lord. The blood shall be a sign for you, on the houses where you are. And when I see the blood, I will pass over you, and no plague will befall you to destroy you, when I strike the land of Egypt. (Ex. 12:11–13)

God was in the process of delivering his people from slavery in Egypt. He was unleashing his almighty power to redeem his people from the trauma they had suffered over four hundred years. His final act of deliverance would be to strike dead the firstborn of every house in Egypt—except those of Israelites who painted blood on the doorposts. In a sign of redeeming grace, God would pass over those houses, and the children of Israel would live and be delivered out of slavery.

When the disciples gather with Jesus to observe the Passover, they have no expectation that anything will be different from how the Jewish people have celebrated the feast for generations. But that night everything they understand about the Passover changes:

> Now as they were eating, Jesus took bread, and after blessing it broke it and gave it to the disciples, and said, "Take, eat; this is my body." And he took a cup, and when he had given thanks he gave it to them, saying, "Drink of it, all of you, for this is my blood of the covenant,

which is poured out for many for the forgiveness of sins. I tell you I will not drink again of this fruit of the vine until that day when I drink it new with you in my Father's kingdom." (Matt. 26:26–29)

With these words, Jesus tells his disciples that the very first Passover and every Passover since had pointed to him. He wants them to know that there is a deeper form of slavery than the physical slavery that their ancestors had experienced. This slavery is infinitely more tragic and causes infinitely more suffering than the Egyptian slavery. And this slavery is universal; no one escapes it. This deeper slavery is the slavery of every heart of every human being to sin. Jesus wants his disciples to know that every lamb of sacrifice was pointing to him. Jesus is saying, "I am the final Lamb of sacrifice, and by my death I will break the power of sin and purchase forgiveness for all who trust in me."

The bad news all of us have to face is that sin captures us all. It always enslaves and leads to death. The good news is that Jesus is the Passover Lamb who has purchased our freedom and our forgiveness. We do well to put our trust in him.

REFLECTION

How has Jesus already freed you from sins in your life? Reflect on the work yet to be done, and pray for Jesus to continue that work by his Spirit and his word.

PRAYER

O Lord, I confess that, like the Egyptians of old, I deserve death. I deserve to be punished for my sin. I do not deserve to be passed over. But I revel in the rich mercy and forgiveness you have shown me in Christ! I rejoice that you did pass over me and my sins, visiting them upon the Lord Jesus Christ instead at the cross. Thank you for freeing me from slavery to sin because of his atoning death and powerful resurrection. In his name I pray, amen.

DAY 24

JOHN 17:1–26

If someone were to ask you how much God loves you, what would you say?

In the middle of talking online with her grandma, our almost three-year-old granddaughter asked to talk to me. When she saw my face on the phone, she smiled wide and began to babble away. I understood about half of what she said. Eventually I told her I needed to get off the phone, but, before I did, I told her that I loved her. With a big grin she said, "I love you too, Grandpa." Those few seconds of life were deeply meaningful to both of us. A young little girl and a not-so-young man both hunger for love, and something happens in our hearts when we hear the words I love you.

The hunger to be loved is universal. It unites all human beings, no matter who they are or where they live. This hunger has been wired into our hearts by our Creator. He built us with this hunger, and he pulls us into a loving relationship with him and into loving community with one another. But now our hunger for love also produces fear. Not only do we hunger for love, but we anxiously wonder whether those who say they love us will continue to love us once they get to know us. If we wonder about this in human relationships, how much more do we wonder about this in our relationship with God? How much does God love us? Does his love have limits? Is his love really a faithful, patient, and forever love? Does he ever break his bond of commitment to us? Does God ever regret that he chose to place his love on us? Does his anger with our sin ever get in the way of his love for us?

All these questions are answered in a few words in the middle of one of Jesus's final recorded prayers. In John 17 Jesus prays for the unity of his followers. He speaks of his love in a way that should bring eternal rest and peace to our hearts: "I in them and you in me, that they may become perfectly one, so that the world may know that you sent me and loved them even as you loved me" (John 17:23). This statement of God's love for us is almost too glorious to fit into our finite human brains. It is so unlike any other experience of love we have ever had that we cannot fully grasp its beauty or extent. The heavenly Father's love for us is the same as his love for his Son, the Lord Jesus. The joy he has in the Son, he has in us. The eternal commitment he has to the Son, he has to us. The unbreakable affection he has for the Son, he has for us. We cannot fully understand God's love for us by simply comparing it to human love. If you want to understand how much God loves you, meditate on his love for his Son. God's love for you is at no greater risk than his love for his Son, and that is the best of news.

REFLECTION

In what ways is the Father's love for the Son—and their love for us—evident in this prayer? Reflect on the depth of the Father's love for his people.

PRAYER

Almighty Lord, who attends faithfully to the prayers of his people, what could I do besides echo the prayer that your Son offered to you so many centuries ago, on the night in which he was betrayed? God, I pray that we your people would become one, just as you the triune God are one. I pray that the world would know Jesus and the love that sent him to earth. Thank you for loving your people in Jesus. I pray in his sweet name, amen.

DAY 25

LUKE 22:31–62

Jesus would not exercise his power to protect himself, and he would not let his disciples defend him, because he came to provide salvation through his suffering and death.

The last week of Jesus's life provides a powerful picture for us of divine, redemptive restraint. The King of kings and Lord of lords, who had legions of angels and infinite power at his disposal, submitted himself to human rejection, betrayal, injustice, and torture till death. Though as the Son of God Jesus had the right to defend himself, he did not exercise his power to do so. He didn't allow his disciples to act for his protection, either. However, as Jesus meekly and willingly submitted to his redemptive calling, he was, in fact, exercising divine power. All of us would have broken at some point. All of us would have been able to bear only so much. All of us would have tried to escape or to fight in our own defense. But in Jesus's last days, there wasn't even a moment of self-preservation. Even when wishing that the cup of suffering would pass by him, he did not seek escape and did not exercise his power to preserve his own life. Jesus never had a moment of self-regarding anger. He exercised divine restraint for the salvation of those who would believe down through the ages. Jesus chose not to defend himself, no matter the cost to himself, because he knew his Father's will and his love for the lost.

In chapter 22, Luke graphically captures this for us:

> "I tell you that this Scripture must be fulfilled in me: 'And he was numbered with the transgressors.' For what is written about me has its fulfillment."

> While he was still speaking, there came a crowd, and the man called Judas, one of the twelve, was leading them. He drew near to Jesus to kiss him, but Jesus said to him, "Judas, would you betray the Son of Man with a kiss?" And when those who were around him saw what would follow, they said, "Lord, shall we strike with the sword?" And one of them struck the servant of the high priest and cut off his right ear. But Jesus said, "No more of this!" And he touched his ear and healed him. Then Jesus said to the chief priests and officers of the temple and elders, who had come out against him, "Have you come out as against a robber, with swords and clubs? When I was with you day after day in the temple, you did not lay hands on me. But this is your hour, and the power of darkness." (Luke 22:37, 47–53)

Jesus understood the eternal plan of redemption. He knew the cross was his destiny, and he was willing. On the Mount of Olives, where he had gone to pray, he did not allow his disciples to take up arms in his defense. He submitted to arrest and to all the suffering that followed. This was a display not of Jesus's weakness but of his divine power. He was in control, fulfilling everything that had been planned and promised, all for our salvation.

REFLECTION

Why do you think Jesus wished the cup of suffering to pass from him? What does it mean to you that he drank that cup anyway?

PRAYER

My Lord, of all that I could be grateful for, there is nothing greater than this: that Jesus would willingly go to the cross to redeem sinners such as I. I am awestruck by his humility, by his power, and by his willing submission to your plan, even unto death. I praise you for all that he has accomplished for my salvation. I thank you for Jesus, as I pray now in his name, amen.

DAY 26

LUKE 23:1–25

Jesus was willing to suffer injustice, mockery, and rejection so that we might experience eternal acceptance.

My daughter had gone to a roller-skating party with a group of her school friends. She had gotten a ride there but would need a ride home, so we told her to call us when she was ready, and we would pick her up. When she eventually called, she asked us not to come in but to stay in the car in the parking lot, and she would come and find us. We knew what was happening. She didn't want to be seen with us. We knew this was typical teenager stuff, but I would be lying to you if I told you it didn't hurt. It is hurtful when someone you love is embarrassed to be identified with you.

God designed us to be social beings, so we hunger for acceptance. We are made for community with other human beings. We all have hearts that cry out for love. None of us enjoys rejection. None of us feels good about being mocked or being the outsider. Isaiah 53 prophesied that Jesus would be despised and rejected. Being fully human, having feelings and desires like you and I have, means that this was painful for Jesus, as it is for us. But Jesus was willing. He knew what he had come to do, and he was willing to suffer so that sin would be defeated and we would be eternally reconciled to God. Luke 23:18–25 records one of those rejection scenes in the life of Jesus:

> They all cried out together, "Away with this man, and release to us Barabbas"—a man who had been thrown into prison for an insurrection started in the city and for murder. Pilate addressed them once more, desiring to release Jesus, but they kept shouting, "Crucify, crucify him!" A third time he said to them, "Why, what evil has

> he done? I have found in him no guilt deserving death. I will therefore punish and release him." But they were urgent, demanding with loud cries that he should be crucified. And their voices prevailed. So Pilate decided that their demand should be granted. He released the man who had been thrown into prison for insurrection and murder, for whom they asked, but he delivered Jesus over to their will.

This scene is so heart-wrenching that it is hard to wrap your brain around it. Perfect Jesus, free of guilt of any kind, was in the legal hands of Pilate, who found no wrong in him. But the crowd wanted Pilate to convict Jesus and release the insurrectionist murderer Barabbas. Think about it: the crowd chose a violent criminal rather than the eternally perfect Son of God.

This moment of public rejection was not a failure of God's plan. No, it was God's plan, prophesied generations before. It was a necessary step toward the victory of Jesus's substitutionary death on the cross. Jesus was willing to do everything necessary, no matter how painful, to accomplish his mission of redemption. His rejection was a step toward gaining our eternal acceptance. Today, for each of us, that's very good news.

REFLECTION

Why did the crowds want Jesus to be crucified? Why is this ironic in light of Jesus's true identity and mission?

PRAYER

Righteous God, I confess that, because of my sin, I deserve to be rejected by you. I deserve to be cut off from your presence eternally, doomed to everlasting punishment merited by my wickedness and rebellion. But I cling to the gospel of Jesus Christ, who was rejected and estranged because of my sin—and who accepted this willingly, out of love for you and for me. Thank you for this incredible news. In Jesus's name, amen.

DAY 27

MARK 15:19–32

Even when he was tortured and mocked,
Jesus exercised divine power on our behalf.

This moment in the final days of Jesus might seem, on the surface, to be a moment of defeat:

> The soldiers led him away inside the palace (that is, the governor's headquarters), and they called together the whole battalion. And they clothed him in a purple cloak, and twisting together a crown of thorns, they put it on him. And they began to salute him, "Hail, King of the Jews!" And they were striking his head with a reed and spitting on him and kneeling down in homage to him. And when they had mocked him, they stripped him of the purple cloak and put his own clothes on him. And they led him out to crucify him. (Mark 15:16–20)

You might read this and think, Where was Jesus's power? Why didn't he do something? Why did he just stand there and take the abuse? Some looked at this moment and concluded that this couldn't be the Son of God, the promised Messiah. Why didn't Jesus call down an army of angels to deal with these blasphemous torturers? How could he let them mock his divine kingship?

But we know that this was far from a moment of weakness. Jesus was not weakly succumbing to humans who hated him and wanted to harm him. No, in this moment Jesus was committed to his eternal redemptive plan; he knew exactly what he was doing. He refused to be diverted. He did not rise to his own defense. He did not let mockery or physical pain cause him to abandon his substitutionary mission. He did not come to earth for his own pleasure, comfort, or acclaim. He could not give in and save himself, because through his suffering he would deliver salvation to multitudes. Jesus's response to this torture did not mock his identity; it was his identity (see Isaiah 53).

You and I should see through the apparent weakness and be blown away by Jesus's divine power. Rather than a show of defeat and weakness, what we witness here is a display of redemptive victory and strength. Jesus knew that his suffering was part of the plan that his Father had established before the world began. He knew the glory of grace that his suffering would unleash. He stood there with the worshiping multitudes in mind, the redeemed from all times and from every tongue and nation. He endured the torture and mockery for you and me. What appeared to be a defeat was another step in the success of his great redemptive mission. Jesus's power was on display, and his power is our hope.

Now, by grace, that same power is ours as the children of God. We stand in both his power and his victory. In him we have the power to stand true in the face of mockery and suffering. When we are mocked, we do not have to be afraid or retaliate, but we can do what Jesus did. We can commend ourselves into the care of our heavenly Father, knowing that he will vindicate us in the end.

REFLECTION

How is Jesus's power a source of hope for sinners like us?

PRAYER

Thank you, heavenly Father, for the cross. Thank you for your Son's victory over death, over evil, over sin, over Satan. Thank you for nailing my iniquities to that tree. May I find my strength in Jesus's work there. And fill my soul with awe at the one who displayed his redemptive victory and strength in such a way, to suffer for me and all those whom he would draw to himself. I pray in his precious name, amen.

DAY 28

MATTHEW 27:45–54

On our behalf, Jesus took every ounce of the Father's rejection.

Matthew 27 records a terrible and dark moment of suffering for Jesus as he hung on the cross:

> Now from the sixth hour there was darkness over all the land until the ninth hour. And about the ninth hour Jesus cried out with a loud voice, saying, "Eli, Eli, lema sabachthani?" that is, "My God, my God, why have you forsaken me?" And some of the bystanders, hearing it, said, "This man is calling Elijah." And one of them at once ran and took a sponge, filled it with sour wine, and put it on a reed and gave it to him to drink. But the others said, "Wait, let us see whether Elijah will come to save him." And Jesus cried out again with a loud voice and yielded up his spirit. (Matt. 27:45–50)

The physical darkness that enveloped the earth for three hours signified how dark that time on the cross truly was. Yes, the scourging of Jesus was horrible, and it is impossible to imagine the pain he experienced when they drove nails through his hands and then hoisted him onto the cross like a cut of beef. None of that physical pain, however, came close to the trauma Jesus went through when he cried, "Eli, Eli, lema sabachthani?" But that horribly dark and painful moment was at the same time a moment of glorious, undeserved grace.

Jesus lived a perfect life as our substitute. In our place, he faced all the temptations that we face, yet without sin. Then he hung on the cross as our substitute, carrying the heavy load of our sin. He hung there, willingly taking the punishment that we deserved. But as he experienced our rejection, he cried out in emotional and spiritual agony. It seems unthinkable that the Father would ever separate himself from the Son. And the Trinity cannot be separated. But in these words, the man Jesus testified to the fact that, for our redemption, he was separated from the Father: "My God, my God, why have you forsaken me?"

Jesus came to earth knowing his job description. He knew that he was coming as the sacrificial Lamb. He knew there would be a decisive redemptive moment when the Father would not exercise his almighty power to come to his rescue. As a man Jesus would hang between heaven and earth, utterly forsaken and alone, rejected not just by his fellow man, but by his heavenly Father. This was necessary so that what was impossible for us to accomplish on our own would be God's gift to us: sin defeated, forgiveness granted, and reconciliation accomplished.

Jesus's humanity endured the Father's rejection so that the children of his grace never would. He was willing to be left utterly alone, so that we would never be alone. He endured the full extent of the Father's anger, so that his anger would never fall on us again. Celebrate today that, as a child of God, you will never be forsaken. Hanging between heaven and earth, Jesus settled that once and for all. His redeeming love for you will never be broken.

REFLECTION

Have you ever felt rejected by God? How is today's reading a deep assurance that in fact God will never reject those with faith in Jesus?

PRAYER

Dear Father, I rejoice in awe at the work of my Savior. I cannot imagine the agony and pain he suffered on behalf of his chosen and precious people. I cannot fathom how he could choose to endure such misery for my sake. And yet he did, and for that I am eternally grateful. Thank you for defeating sin and granting forgiveness and reconciliation through his suffering. In his name, amen.

DAY 29

PSALM 22:1–31

The Bible graphically depicts the hardships of life in this fallen world, assuring us that God sees, knows, and understands our suffering.

When suffering enters our door—when we are weakened and distressed by the unexpected, the unplanned, the unwanted—we are susceptible to listening to the lies of the enemy. One lie is that we have been singled out; that is, that our suffering is unique. This is the lie that God has favorites, and we are not one of them. Another lie comes in the form of a question: "Where is your God now?" This is the lie that God has abandoned us and doesn't always keep his promises. In our moments of weakness, the enemy wants us to doubt the love, goodness, and covenant faithfulness of the Lord. The enemy knows that when we begin to doubt God's goodness, we stop going to him for help. And if we doubt the love of God, then we won't follow him by faith.

In its honesty about the dangers, hardships, and trials of life, the Bible silences these lies. Over and over, the Bible shows us the struggles of people like you and me. Scripture doesn't give us a sanitized depiction of life, one free of disappointments and hardships. This assures us that God sees, knows, understands, and cares about what we are going through. He reminds us that his promises do not depict some unreal world that none of us live in. Rather, he gives us hope in the middle of the real world of hardship. One place where the cries of the sufferer are graphically depicted is Psalm 22:

> My God, my God, why have you forsaken me?
> Why are you so far from saving me, from the words of my groaning?

O my God, I cry by day, but you do not answer,
  and by night, but I find no rest. . . .
I am poured out like water,
  and all my bones are out of joint;
my heart is like wax;
  it is melted within my breast;
my strength is dried up like a potsherd,
  and my tongue sticks to my jaws;
  you lay me in the dust of death. (Ps. 22:1–2, 14–15)

Psalm 22 not only accurately depicts our struggles in times of hardship; it also welcomes us to take our cries to our Lord. Jesus applies this psalm to himself, reminding us that he is one with us in our suffering (Matt. 27:46; Heb. 5:7). But there is more. Jesus came to earth, willing to suffer on our behalf, to purchase for us the guarantee that someday we would suffer no more. In him we find comfort as we suffer now and hope for a future when we will be free from suffering forever.

REFLECTION

Consider all the various ways that Jesus's suffering, death, and resurrection fulfill the patterns established in Psalm 22. Reflect on Jesus's willingness to endure all these things for the sake of his people.

PRAYER

O Lord, do not be far off! O God my help, come quickly to my aid! As the psalmist prays, so do I. Thank you for seeing me in my distress and coming to my rescue. Thank you that Jesus came to earth to endure the suffering that my sin deserved, dying in my place and rising for my everlasting life and joy. I pray in his name, amen.

DAY 30

REVELATION 19:1–16

The biblical story begins and ends with a meal.

I have to confess that I love food. I love the beauty of a well-dressed plate. I love the smells of something slowly roasting in the oven. I love the sizzle of something frying on the stove. I love the chemistry of food, how heat changes it and how spices enhance flavor. I do the cooking in our family. I love designing and preparing the Thanksgiving and Christmas meals. We have a large market nearby, with about a hundred vendors. Every kind of food you could want is there, along with butchers, fishmongers, and fresh produce. I walk through the market almost every day. I call it my food museum. I also love how much the biblical writers incorporate food into their narratives, and often use it as a metaphor of the work of God.

It is striking that the grand biblical story is bracketed by two meals. The first meal is the most tragic meal that has ever been eaten. High drama precedes this meal, as Satan tempts Eve and Adam to eat something God has forbidden. As you listen to the serpent's seductive lies, you think, "Don't listen!" And, as they take the forbidden fruit into their hands, you want to scream, "Don't eat; don't eat!" But they do. This first recorded meal is an act of outrageous rebellion against God's authority, warning, and loving provision. When the first bite is taken, the history of the world goes dark. Not only does sin enter the hearts of Adam and Eve, but it spreads its destructive power around the cosmos. This meal is a tragedy, and humanity still suffers its effects today.

But, thankfully, the redemptive story marches toward another meal. This one is not a tragedy, but a victory. It is a meal not of rebellion but of divine love. The beauty and glory of this meal is captured in Revelation 19: "I heard what seemed to be the voice of a great multitude, like the roar of many waters and like the sound of mighty peals of thunder, crying out, 'Hallelujah! For the Lord our God the Almighty reigns'" (Rev. 19:6).

Open your heart and expand your imagination to take in this scene. This is your guaranteed destiny as a child of God. It is a royal marriage processional. The reigning Lamb takes us as his bride, now pure before him and with him forever. The angel says to John, "Write this: Blessed are those who are invited to the marriage supper of the Lamb" (Rev. 19:9). This is Scripture's final meal. Sin has been defeated. There will be no more rebellious meals. The eternal celebration has begun. The children of God have been forever united to the Lamb. Redemption has been accomplished. God has won!

REFLECTION

How do the words of the songs recorded in Revelation 19 both reflect upon Jesus's death and resurrection and also cause us to look ahead with anticipation of his return?

PRAYER

Hallelujah! Indeed, Lord God Almighty—you reign! I rejoice and exult and give you the glory. I delight in the eternal marriage between us, the church, and our bridegroom—the Lamb, the Lord Jesus Christ. Thank you for his power and his righteousness that have allowed us to make ourselves ready; thank you for granting us to clothe ourselves with fine linen, bright and pure. Thank you for Jesus. In his name, amen.

PAUL TRIPP MINISTRIES

Paul Tripp Ministries is a not-for-profit organization connecting the transforming power of Jesus Christ to everyday life. Supported by generous donors, they make much of Paul's gospel teaching freely available online, on podcasts, across social media, and in the Paul Tripp app.

PaulTripp.com

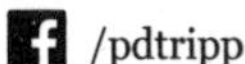

@paultrippquotes

Also Available from the Everyday Gospel Suite

Paul David Tripp's Everyday Gospel suite helps you connect the transforming power of Scripture to everyday life. Featuring 365 theologically rich and practical daily devotions that follow an annual Bible reading plan, these resources encourage you to spend time in God's word every day and apply the gospel's life-changing truths all year long.

For more information, visit **crossway.org** or **paultripp.com**.